Five Children and It

Adapted by Marietta Kirkbride

Original song lyrics by
Marietta Kirkbride and David Ridley

T0284165

methuen | drama

LONDON • NEW YORK • OXFORD • NEW DELHI • SYDNEY

METHUEN DRAMA
Bloomsbury Publishing Plc
50 Bedford Square, London, WC1B 3DP, UK
1385 Broadway, New York, NY 10018, USA
29 Earlsfort Terrace, Dublin 2, Ireland

BLOOMSBURY, METHUEN DRAMA and the Methuen
Drama logo are trademarks of Bloomsbury Publishing Plc

First published in Great Britain 2023

Series design: Rebecca Heselton

Cover image: Feathers © Potapov Alexander/Shutterstock

A catalogue record for this book is available from the British Library.

A catalog record for this book is available from the Library of Congress.

ISBN: PB: 978-1-3504-2312-1
ePDF: 978-1-3504-2313-8
eBook: 978-1-3504-2314-5

Series: Plays for Young People

Typeset by Mark Heslington Ltd, Scarborough, North Yorkshire

To find out more about our authors and books visit
www.bloomsbury.com and sign up for our newsletters.

Five Children and It

Written by Marietta Kirkbride

Song lyrics by Marietta Kirkbride and David Ridley

Adapted from the novel by E. Nesbit

Production Credits

Five Children and It was a Bucket Club production first presented by The Egg at Theatre Royal Bath in December 2021, and then again in December 2022.

The cast and creatives who made this production and its remount were as follows:

Friday 10 December 2021–Sunday 16 January 2022

It	**Craig Edwards**
Jane	**Hanora Kamen**
Cyril	**Luke Murphy**
Anthea	**Doxah Dzidzor**
Robert	**Hannah Bristow**
Uncle Paul	**Patrick Bridgman**
It / Uncle Paul / Cyril (understudy)	**Peta Maurice**
Jane / Anthea / Robert (understudy)	**Dixie Newman**

Director	Nel Crouch
Writer	Marietta Kirkbride
Designer	Rebecca Wood
Composer, Sound Designer, MD	David Ridley
Lighting Designer	Joe Price
Movement Director	Jennifer Jackson
Associate Designer	Sophie Thomas
Puppet Director	Aya Nakamura
Production Manager	Lisa Hall
Costume Supervisor & Wardrobe	Anna Dixon
Company Stage Manager	Jess Pomeroy
Deputy Stage Manager	Kirsty Milne
Assistant Stage Management	Amy Palmer, Helena Walker, Paul Sage
Wardrobe Assistant	Rebecca Hughes
Set Builder	Sam Raine at Future Carpentry Services
Scenic artist	Nina Raine
Puppet Maker	Cat Rock

Friday 9 December 2022–Sunday 15 January 2023

It	**Rose Wardlaw**
Jane	**Kezrena James**
Cyril	**Joseph Tweedale**
Anthea	**Tika Mu'Tamir**
Robert	**Ellie Showering**
Uncle Paul	**Patrick Bridgman**
It / Uncle Paul / Cyril (understudy)	**Peta Maurice**
Jane / Anthea / Robert (understudy)	**Dixie Newman**

Director	Nel Crouch
Writer	Marietta Kirkbride
Designer	Rebecca Wood
Composer, Sound Designer, MD	David Ridley
Lighting Designer	Joe Price
Movement Director	Jennifer Jackson
Assistant Director	Lex Kaby
Production Manager	Lisa Hall
Costume Supervisor & Wardrobe	Anna Dixon
Company Stage Manager	Kirsty Milne
Deputy Stage Manager	Chaz Webb
Assistant Stage Management	Lauren Stone-Symes, Rachel O'Connell

For *Five Children and It* the producing team at The Egg were: Kate Cross, Lindsay Baker, Tim Bell and Nik Partridge.

Bucket Club are produced by Farnham Maltings, where this project was supported by Laura Woodward.

Writer and Director's Note

There is something joyous about coming back to a story you loved as a child and re-reading it as an adult. It's like opening a treasure box. There is all the fairy gold you dimly remembered as well as new diamonds the child 'you' couldn't see.

What we both loved about E. Nesbit's *Five Children and It* is how naughty her narrative voice is. A lifelong non-conformist, committed socialist and a deep thinker on the inner lives of children, she rebukes and teases her reader as an equal. The story is littered with quips and self-referential asides:

'And that, my dear children, is the moral of this chapter. I did not mean it to have a moral, but morals are nasty forward beings, and will keep putting in their oars where they are not wanted.'

Gold! But how to bring this into the play?

Growing up in the 1990s, we were exposed to the BBC TV adaptation of the book with its creepy puppet Sandfairy. When we, as Bucket Club, started talking about adapting this story for stage, we'd turn to each other and say: 'But ours won't be like the TV "It", yeah?' So what would our 'It' be? As we started developing ideas we found in 'It' a natural home for everything we loved about E. Nesbit: impulsive, cheeky, god-like, daft. We hope you enjoy It, and sorry in advance if It gives your audiences a hard time.

When adapting something there will always be elements you cannot capture, details that are less tantalising or simply no longer relevant. These have lost their place in the jostle for a spot in our play. Nesbit's *Five Children and It* was originally written as a serial for weekly publication. By its nature it is episodic which, structurally, can feel formulaic and stale in a piece of theatre, and there are times where the original characters feel trapped by the rigid gender expectations of the era they were created in.

In this play we have looked for the children E. Nesbit might have written if she were writing them now. And for the story, we have built a new narrative arc by adapting a plot line from Nesbit's *The Railway Children*. You'll see we have shifted the time setting slightly from 1902 to the more politically-charged end of the Edwardian era in 1910. We did this because when we first created the show in 2021, we were still recovering as artists – and people – from all the shocks of the year before. What we've all experienced since the pandemic in 2020 is that the world can change overnight. The rug of routine can be pulled from our feet at a moment's notice. Rules are changed or broken. In the past three years, shocking acts of race and gender violence have prompted protest and demand for social change around the world. So it is for us now and so it is for the Edwardian children in our play. But this story is also joyful. It is full of magic and silliness and redemption. We hope you have as much fun with this play as we did when we made it.

From Writer, Marietta Kirkbride, and Director, Nel Crouch, 2023

Acknowledgements

Thank you to Kate Cross for her genius insights, to Lindsay and the whole team at The Egg for working tirelessly to make this play happen through the covid mayhem. To Nik Partridge, Tim Bell and Laura Woodward.

A huge shout out to our wider Bucket Club family – Adam Farrell, Matt Lister, Katie Sherrard, Helen Cooper, Becky Ripley, Emily Tate, Aaron May, Letty Thomas, Cassie Harrison, you're all part of this journey. My personal thanks also go to writing friends Marek Horn, Miriam Battye, Charlotte Spires and Bea Roberts for their support and advice along my writing journey – I've needed it. And thanks to Sharon Clark for teaching me to write in the first place.

To my parents and brothers – I've thought of you often with love whilst writing this play. And to Andy – thank you for everything.

Finally, extra special thanks to Bex, Dave and Nel for your friendship, inspiration and generous collaborative spirit. Nel, this play is for you. Not a single word would have been written had it not been for you.

M.K.

Five Children and It

Characters

It, *ageless, genderless, an agent of chaos*
Jane, *aged 12, principled, determined, political*
Cyril, *aged 10, fussy, paternal, earnest*
Anthea, *aged 8, wild, earthy, thoughtful*
Robert, *aged 7, quick tempered, excitable, keen sense of justice*
Uncle Paul, *a farmer, gruff, kind*

Other Characters

Played by same actor as **It***:*

Driver, *owner of a pony and trap*
Baker / **Book Seller** / **Hat Seller** / **Butcher**, *unhelpful owners of shops*
Billy Peasemarsh, *proud, a trader of horses*
Megan, *alarming, the vicar's assistant – if* **It** *is played by a male actor,* **Megan** *should be male and called* **Andrew**
Hilary, *flamboyant and entitled,* **The Lamb** *grown up*
Wulfric de Talbot, *terrifying, a leader of knights*

Played by same actor as **Uncle Paul***:*

Inspector, *stoic, a police inspector*
Vicar, *gentle*
Lady Artist, *dashing, snobbish*
Jakin, *a fearsome knight*

Minions, *in our production, the actors playing the children also played instruments during* **It**'s *songs. This led them to taking on a wider dramaturgical role as* **It**'s *'minions' – an ensemble of aloof, voiceless beings who act as a sort of extension of* **It** *and are subservient to* **It**'s *on stage needs.*

The Lamb, *the children's baby brother, was a bundle.*

In our production, in Act Two, we swapped **Hilary**'s *Edwardian bicycle for a scooter.*

Notes

Indented text represents song lyrics.

A forward slash (/) indicates overlapping dialogue; it indicates when the next character should start speaking.

The children in this play should not be played childishly. They take themselves completely seriously in the same way adults do.

The performance of **It** *should feel intensely, wildly live.* **It***'s interactions with the audience should be partly improvised and audience led.*

Act One

It and The Audience (A Show)

It *is asleep, buried up to its neck in a large mound of rubble and sand.*

It *wakes up with a start – perhaps it is woken by a* **Minion**.

It   Arghhh!

Okay okay okay okay. Humans. Human beings and their . . .

It *sniffs.*

Ch – . . . Chil – . . . Chil –

Children.

It *eyeballs a child in the audience with trepidation.*

It *recovers.*

All sitting in rows. In the dark. That is very strange behaviour. What are they all doing, are they . . .?

(*To an adult in the audience.*) You. That one. Yes, you. Where am I? (**It** *asks this sincerely until the answer 'a theatre' is given.*) A what? A th – thhh – a 'theatre'? Okay. And that's what humans do in a theatre, is it? They sit in rows and stare in one direction? Right.

But why are there so many chi – . . . chil –?

(*To self, as if uttering a curse.*) Children.

Okay. Wishes. Okay. I'm good at wishes. I can do wishes.

(*To a child member of the audience.*) You. Child. Bet you'd love to have a wish granted, wouldn't you? Go on then, what is it? What would you wish for?

(**It** *asks a few different children what they'd wish for.* **It** *considers wishes that are too practical or typical to be boring and tedious. Wishes that spark chaos or joy are good wishes. Wishes containing human concepts or anything too modern are wishes that* **It** *must grant but doesn't understand.*)

Alright. But I can't do much about any of these while I'm like this, can I? One of you will have to finish digging me up. Who here's good at digging?

A **Minion** *presents an audience member with a small spade.*

It   Come on then. But don't go anywhere near my whiskers. Okay?

Audience member comes to stage. **It** *instructs them how to dig it up. Perhaps like this:*

Right so see my friend here (**Minion**.)? You're going to dig me up together. Do as they do. And the rest of you, we're going to need your help. If there's anything children are good at, it's making a racket, so shout: dig, dig, dig! Come on. Come on.

The audience chant 'dig'. **It** *is dug up.*

It *thanks the audience member who sits back down.*

Right. So we've had (*Lists some of the wishes.*) Okay. And then . . . Well then there's all the rest of you, aren't there, so . . .

My goodness there's a lot of you. This is going to be . . .

It *trembles.*

No I can't. Sorry. There's just – There's too many of you!

Only one of you gets a wish. Yes. Sorry.

So what we'll do is – to make it fair – you can all close your eyes, each make a wish, and then I'll pick one and grant it. Okay?

Right, so in your head you say: I wish . . . blah blah blah blah. Okay? But you have to say 'I Wish' or it doesn't work. Okay?

So close your eyes then. Go on.

Good.

And wish.

*The audience close their eyes and wish. If anyone speaks, **It** must remind them to say 'I wish' in their heads.*

It *considers the wishes.*

Alright. I've chosen. Here we go.

It *prepares for wish granting. Perhaps this involves some stretching.*

It *grants the wish. This should be a surprising process requiring great focus and effort.*

There.

It *recovers itself.*

So one of you wished for A Show to hurry up and start. Absolutely no idea what Ashow is, but you've got one, and it will hurry up and start very s – sssssssshhhhhaaaaahhhhh

It *is catapulted out of our world and sucked into the world of the play.*

The play begins.

London

London. The Edwardian era.

The Edwardian children storm the stage.

Robert   Anthea!

Anthea   What?

Robert   Put it down.

Anthea   I'm using it, Robert.

*Perhaps **Anthea** has a rolling pin. Perhaps **Robert** tries to take it.*

Anthea   I said I'm using it.

Robert   Well you can't so give it here.

Anthea   No.

Robert   You're rubbish at it.

Cyril   Anthea. Robert. You need to pack.

Robert   I have.

Cyril   You haven't.

Robert   It can wait.

Cyril   It really can't.

Robert   Listen to me. Anthea and I are preparing for a war. Do you really think packing is top of my agenda right now?

Cyril   Call a truce.

Robert   Not possible.

Anthea   The warriors are here!

Cyril   Where's The Lamb's blanket?

Jane   I don't know.

Cyril   Everyone, the train to the countryside leaves in twenty minutes time. That's twenty minutes.

Anthea   I smelleth the blood of mine enemy.

Cyril   And we still have to walk there.

Robert   Charge!

Cyril   Jane, help me?

>   We're going to have the funnest time
>   Where we're going to stay in the countryside (the countryside)
>   Where fields are green and skies are blue
>   So pack your things, your panties too

Robert   Anthea, get the trebuchet.

Anthea   I don't want the trebuchet.

Cyril   Jane, will you take The Lamb?

Jane   What? No!

Cyril   Look, *I* need to pack now, and I can't if I'm watching a stupid baby.

Jane   I'm packing my books.

Cyril   We're away for two weeks. You do not need that many books.

Jane   Just put him on the floor.

Cyril   What?!

Anthea / Robert   Chaaaarge!

> We're going to eat a crumbly pie
> Made by Uncle Paul in the countryside (the countryside)
> We're going to eat a lot of cheese
> Apparently it grows on trees

Cyril   Where's the pram?

Jane   I've got it.

Cyril   Right. If we don't go now we'll miss the train and Mother will never forgive us.

Robert   Urghh! I hate this!

Anthea   Jane?

Jane   What?

Anthea   Found this by the door. It's got your name on it.

Anthea *hands* **Jane** *an envelope.*

Jane   It's a note from Mother.

Anthea   About The Cause?

Jane   Don't know. I'll read it later.

Robert   Why don't I have a note?

Cyril   Everyone. Station.

Robert   Cyril got instructions and Jane got a note. Where's my thing?

Cyril   Doesn't matter. Let's go.

> It'll be a rather bumpy ride
> Unless we catch the train to the countryside (the country side)
> We've never been on a train before
> Quick, now run to platform four

Cyril   Quick. Everyone on. Bags on.

The children tumble onto a train.

Anthea   The Lamb!

Cyril   Oh!

The Lamb *was almost forgotten. Awkward scramble to get the pram on too.*

Robert   Right. Where's the picnic?

Cyril   Not yet. We need to save it as emergency rations. In case we – Anthea!

Anthea *is eating an apple from the picnic. The picnic is breached.*

> We're going to the countryside
> 'Til Mother sorts things out
> We'll fish for trout and capture bears
> We'll feast on cake and juicy pears.

Anthea   I think we're here.

The children tumble off the train.

All   The countryside!

The heavens open. Epic rain.

The children pick up their bags and trudge miserably through the rain.

The Farm

Uncle Paul, *in a big wet coat and covered in mud, is milking a cow called Rosie. He is in his element. He sings to himself as he works. Perhaps he has a surprisingly impressive voice.*

Paul   I live in the countryside
In the rain and mud

Rosie the cow moos.

Paul   Alright Rosie.

I love the peace and quiet here
The city stress is nowhere near

Anthea   Nice singing!

Uncle Paul *leaps up in shock.*

Cyril *(formally)*   Hello, sorry to interrupt your singing but we're looking for Mr Uncle Paul. He owns this farm. Do you know him?

Paul   They've come, Rosie.

Cyril   Sorry?

Paul   It's them.

Robert   Is he talking to a cow?

Paul   They're bigger though, girl. My goodness there's a lot of them.

Robert   He is!

Cyril   Right. Let's – Let's go.

Paul   Jane?

Jane   Yes.

Paul   It is, it's little Jane. You must have been thirty pounds last time I seen you. And now look at you. Nearly the weight of a full grown ewe.

Cyril   Are you Uncle Paul?

Paul   I am. Nice to . . . You know.

The children look at each other. This wasn't what they imagined.

Cyril (*offering a hand*)   Cyril. And this is Robert, and Anthea, who we call Panther. And – well you know Jane. And that's The Lamb who's really called Hilary but no one calls him that because that would be ridiculous.

Paul   Right.

Robert   Could we have some dinner, Uncle Paul? Sorry if that's forward, but I'm genuinely starving.

Anthea   Me too.

Paul   Oh. Well there's no dinner yet. Not till the chores are all done.

Robert   Right. And when is that?

Paul   It's when the chores are all done.

Cyril (*chortles to the others*)   Country humour. (*Helpfully.*) We have dinner at one o'clock in London.

Paul   Well out here it's when the sheep are moved, the cows milked, the pigs fed, and the eggs collected. But between the lot of us we'll have that done in no time. So, you can start with forking the hay, you can feed chickens, and –

Anthea   Can't I feed the chickens?

Paul   Well – Alright. Then you can muck out pigs, and you'll look after the baby since you're –

Jane   No!

Paul   What?

Jane   I won't be lumped with the baby, just cos I'm a girl.

Paul   Oh.

Jane   He cries non-stop, he farts on my clothes.

The children talk over each other protesting their jobs.

Jane   / I've had to change him twice today and the smell of poo is following me everywhere – like a bad smell, literally. It's disgusting. (*Etc.*)

Cyril   / Hay is actually really bad for my eczema. I get very itchy. Itchy all over. Rashes. Scabs. It's terrible, so if I could do something else that doesn't involve (*Etc.*)

Robert   / I shall keel over and die if I muck out pigs before dinner. I shall die of thirst and famine. You can't do that to me, it's child cruelty. You'll be thrown into prison (*Etc.*)

Anthea   / Where are the chickens? I'll help with the chickens. If there's a rooster I'd like to take a tail feather for my collection please. I have a feather collection but the birds aren't so good in the city, so I (*Etc.*)

Paul   STOP! Listen to you. Why did your mother have to bring you up in London, eh? Look at what's become of you. Bunch of spoilt city kids. Put your bags in the house and go occupy yourselves. A farm doesn't run itself, you know. Come on, Rosie.

Uncle Paul *goes, taking his cow.*

Robert   This is even worse than I could possibly have imagined.

Cyril   If we can't eat we'll have to distract ourselves. What do we do?

Anthea   Explore!

The children investigate their surroundings.

The space transforms into . . .

Wishes

. . . *A quarry.*

Anthea   Wow!

Robert   A beach!

Jane   It's not a beach, stupid.

Robert   It is.

Jane   Alright then where's the sea?

Cyril   Maybe it's a quarry.

Jane   Obviously it's a quarry. They're digging for limestone most likely. I read about it.

Robert (*mimicking*)   I read about it.

Well, Jane, I know for a fact you need limes to make limestone. And can you see any limes?

Jane   That's not how it –

Robert   No! Exactly!

Jane *reads her book.*

Anthea   Do snakes live in quarries?

Cyril   I don't know. Probably.

Anthea   I'm going to find an adder.

Cyril   No – Anthea, that's not a good idea!

The Lamb *begins to cry. A frustrated* **Cyril** *tries to hush him.*

Robert   What shall we play then? One of you idiots must have an idea. Squirrel?

But **Cyril** *is trying to calm the baby.*

Robert   Panther?

But **Anthea** *is hunting for snakes.*

Robert   What are you reading, Jane?

Jane   Vindication of the Rights of Woman.

Robert   Oh. Any good?

Jane   Yes actually. Really ahead of its time.

Robert   What's it about?

Jane   Women.

Robert   What about them?

Jane   Stuff.

Robert   Not really reading it, are you?

Jane   I would be if you weren't yakking in my ear, Robert.

. . .

Robert   Fine. I'm digging to Australia. You're boring, you're boring. Anthea is mad and Australia's got to be more interesting than here. Bye.

Jane   Bye then.

Robert   Bye. I need a spade.

A child's spade appears.

Robert *digs for Australia, until* . . .

Robert   Everyone! I think I've found something.

Jane   Shut up.

Robert   No seriously, Jane. Come back and look.

It *is revealed.*

It   What –

Robert   Ahh!

It   Where am I?

Robert   AHHHH!

It   What's going on?

Jane   What?

It (*realising something*)   Oh.

Cyril   Oh my – Joseph-Mary-Mark-and-John.

Anthea   Is it a Python?

Jane   No, it's –

It   Is this A Show?

Anthea   It can speak!

Cyril   Shhh, Panther!

It   Of course I can speak.

Anthea   Where's Ashow?

It   It is, isn't it? It's Ashow and I'm in it.

Anthea   What are you talking about?

Robert   Oh it's horrid.

Jane   Since you can speak, tell us what you are please.

Cyril   Yes, and swear by King Edward you'll speak honestly.

It   But – You know what I am.

The children shake their heads.

It   What? Really?

Robert   I think it's a demon.

Anthea   No it's a new, undiscovered species!

It   I'm a Psammead.

Robert   What?

It   Psammead.

Cyril   That's Greek to me.

It   A – Seriously?

Anthea   What's it saying?

It   Psammead. A Sand Fairy.

Jane   Right. Sure – a fairy.

It   How old are you?

Jane   Twelve.

It   Ahh yes, I know about you.

Jane (*freaked out*)   What?

Anthea   How long have you lived here, Psammead?

It   Don't know. Few thousand years?

Anthea   Wow. That's ages.

It   Is it? Well, after three hundred millennia the centuries do start to flash by.

Anthea   We've only lived here a day.

Robert   Anthea, we don't live here. This is just a holiday.

It   Hhholiday?

Robert   We live in London. With Mother. Remember?

It   Right, all this talking is making my whiskers feel clammy. Hurry up and wish for something or you won't get so much as a pterodactyl sausage.

Cyril   What do you mean?

It   I mean wish! Come on. You're children, you found me, you get wishes. Obviously.

Jane *snorts*.

Robert / **Anthea**   Jane!

Jane   Anyone that finds you gets *wishes*?

It   I have a child only policy.

Jane   Why?

Robert   Jane, shut up.

Jane   Doesn't sound very fair.

Robert   Stop being rude, it'll change its mind.

Cyril   What's the cut off point for being a child?

It   Depends who's asking.

Robert   When will I stop being a child?

It   Forty-five. Look, thing is, human adults don't wish like you do. They want dull, earnest things. Like Sewage Systems. Pensioning Plans. Those Boxy Hedge things.

Robert   What?

It   Exhausting. And of course if adults could wish they'd always be wanting more and more of them. Or they'd find some clever way of making wishes last until after sunset. So then it would be wishes non-stop. Forever. All of life – just one long, agonising wish upon wish upon wish, until my eyestalks sag and my whiskers shrivel and I'm I'm I'm . . .

It *has a meltdown at the thought of ending up as a washed-out, wished-up heap of magical detritus.*

. . .

Cyril   Right, let's get this straight: we found you, we're children and so for that you grant us wishes. And the wishes last until sunset?

It (*resigned*)   Yes, that's it.

Robert   How many do we get?

It   One each.

Robert   Ten each.

It   One a day.

Robert   Deal!

It   Okay. Well, what is it then? What's the wish?

Jane   Well, it's obvious, isn't it? If it can do this – which I'm not saying it can, but if it could – then the wish is to be home with Mother again.

It   Okay –

Robert   No, wait! The wish only lasts for a day, Jane.

Jane   So?

Cyril   No, it's a good point. There's no use wishing for something and then finding ourselves back at square one tomorrow.

Anthea   And if we're home with Mother, that might hold up The Cause. And things can't be normal 'til The Cause is won, remember? That's what she said.

Cyril   Exactly. We should wish for something clever.

Anthea   A pit of lizards!

Robert / Jane / Cyril   No!

Anthea   Fascinating!

It   Right, I'm going.

Robert   I WISH I WAS RICH BEYOND MY WILDEST DREAMS!

It (*stern, a little sinister*)   Alright. But I can't go beyond dreams, you know? Nothing can go beyond dreams.

Will you have it in gold or notes?

Robert   Gold! Millions of it!

It   Right. Stand back.

Cyril   Why?

It *grants the wish. This is a different and more painful process than granting the audience's wish.*

The quarry fills with gold. The children cry out as they hurry to escape it.

At last the creating of the wish stops.

It *has gone.*

The children interact with the gold. It is joyous.

Robert   / I'm rich I'm rich I'm rich I'm rich

Anthea   We're rich we're rich we're rich

Cyril   Gold!

Jane   No.

Cyril   Amazing!

Jane   This isn't possible.

Cyril   I've made my fortune as a man. And I'm only ten!

Anthea   What shall we do with it?

Robert   Spend it!

Anthea   Yes!

Robert   Motorcars. Pocket watch. / Toy soldiers. Treacle tart. Gob stoppers (*Etc.*)

Anthea   / Fishing net. Penknife. Aquarium. Spider crabs. Tree house. Exotic fish (*Etc.*)

Cyril   / Three piece suit – No, investments. Business things. A ship! Or a factory – yes! A lace factory or –

Jane   No. Stop it. Don't you see? If this is real we could really *do* something. We could change the world with this much gold.

Robert   Change it for a day? (*Scoffs.*)

Jane   But we could feed people that are hungry, we could –

Robert   No. The poor can find their own fairy. The gold is mine.

Cyril   We can't just go around giving gold to people.

Jane   Why not?

Cyril   Because – Well I don't know exactly, but I'm sure it's a bad idea.

Jane   How about we have a vote to decide what to do with it.

Robert   Good idea. But Jane? Jane? You're a girl, remember? So you don't get to vote.

Jane *lunges at* **Robert**. *A fight.* **Cyril** *tries to separate them.*

Anthea   Stop it!

Anthea *bursts into tears.*

Jane (*ferocious*)   What?

Anthea   I'm – I'm – I'm – I think I'm hungry.

Cyril   How about this, we get a carriage into a town. We buy steak and kidney pudding, ginger beer, treacle sponge. And after that we'll decide what to do with the gold.

Robert   My gold.

Cyril   Robert's gold. Agreed?

Robert / **Anthea**   Agreed.

Jane   Fine.

Robert / **Cyril** / **Anthea**   To town!

Town

Music. The children fill their pockets with gold and go in search of a carriage.

> We're rich with gold
> Stuff it in your pockets
> It's nice to hold
> Keeps us warm though it's always cold
> We're rich! We're rich!

We'll buy what we like
Steak and kidney pudding for our tums
Cheese and ham and three penny buns
We're rich. We're rich with

Anthea   Fresh horse poo!

Robert   Gross.

Jane   You are disgusting, Panther.

Anthea   No. That means a horse is near.

Driver *appears with his pony and trap.*

Cyril   Hello, sir. I say, would you give us a lift on the back of your cart?

Driver *mumbles something indistinguishable.*

Cyril   We'd like to go to town.

Driver *mumbles something indistinguishable.*

Anthea   We can give you this for payment.

Anthea *hands over a gold coin.* **Driver** *examines it.*

Driver *mumbles something indistinguishable.*

The children shrug and pile on.

Cyril   The Lamb!

One of the children gets **The Lamb**.

Driver *drives. The cart ride is incredibly bumpy and uncomfortable.*

We're rich with gold
Heavy and steady it's weighing us down
Flash that cash. We're off to town
Can't wait, can't wait
To spend it all
Can we save some pennies for the poor?
Who cares we'll never want for more
We're rich. We're rich with

Driver   Woahh.

Jane   Thank you, driver.

Cyril   Thank you, driver.

Anthea   Thank you, driver.

Driver *mumbles something indistinguishable.*

Driver *goes.*

Robert   A bakery.

All   Dinner.

The children pile into the bakery and find **Baker**. **Cyril** *is lumped with* **The Lamb**.

Jane   Please could we have five iced buns, five scones, five eclairs –

Robert   Five gingerbreads

Anthea   And five jam tarts.

Cyril   We can't just eat cake for dinner.

Anthea   Why not?

Jane   And we'll take one sausage roll, thanks.

Here, is that enough?

Baker *inspects it the gold coin.*

Baker   What's that?

Jane   Gold coin.

Baker   Well, that won't get you so much as a biscuit, I'm afraid.

Robert   Ridiculous. It's pure gold. It's worth thousands. You should count yourself lucky to get it.

Baker   Well, you should count yourself lucky I don't send for the police. Where d'you get this?

Robert   It's ours!

Baker   Is it?

Jane   You know, I think I fancy something else for dinner. Thanks for your time, baker.

The children go.

Cyril   That was close.

Jane   There'll be somewhere that accepts gold coin. We've just got to find which shop.

Cyril   Okay. You and Robert go that way and –

Jane / Robert   No thanks.

Cyril   Fine. Just find somewhere that accepts this.

The children split up to investigate gold-accepting shops.

> We're rich with gold
> Shoppy shoppy shops everywhere
> Spend spend spend without a care
> We're rich. We're rich with

Anthea *at a book shop.* **Book Seller** *appears.*

Anthea   Hello. Can I buy this book on British earthworms? I love earthworms. Really wiggly and fascinating, aren't they?

Book Seller   Yes, I'd say so too actually.

Anthea   You know, I have my own wormery.

Book Seller   Really?

Anthea   Yes. Huge one. Around the same size as Buckingham Palace except all underground. Here.

Book Seller   How remarkable. And where is this – (*Noticing gold coin.*) Oh. This is old money you've got here. Do you have anything more current?

Anthea   No actually.

Book Seller   Well. I'm sorry, little girl, but I don't take this.

Anthea   Please?

Book Seller *goes.*

Jane *is at a hat shop admiring a magnificent hat.*

Jane   So on the one hand, spending three guineas on a hat, isn't exactly socialist. But, on the other, I would look excellent in it. And I could always take it off and set it down firmly, like Mother does, to make a point. Maybe if I just . . .

Jane *tries on the hat.* **Jane** *instantly feels like a rock star.*

Hat Seller *appears.*

Hat Seller   Ahem.

Jane   Hello, I'd like to buy this, please.

Hat Seller   I'm afraid that'll be out of your price range, Madam.

Jane   No, I have the means. Here – three guineas.

Hat Seller   Oh no, I can't accept that.

Jane   It's good money!

Hat Seller   But acquired by dishonourable means, no doubt.

Jane   What?

Hat Seller   I won't have trouble makers like you wearing our hats. This isn't that sort of establishment.

Jane   But –

Hat Seller *takes hat and goes.*

Anthea   Get something?

Jane   No.

Anthea   Me neither.

Jane   People seem to think we've stolen the money.

Cyril *and* **Robert** *hurtle across the stage.*

Robert   We don't want your side of lamb anyway! You beef-faced, ham-fisted, string of stupid sausages!

Butcher *appears holding an enormous meat cleaver.*

Cyril *and* **Robert** *hide behind* **Jane** *and* **Anthea**.

Butcher *goes.*

Cyril   This is a disaster.

Jane   Yep.

Robert   That Sand Fairy is wicked.

Cyril   We're stuck here now. And we can't even nibble on a biscuit.

Jane   We should find the cart driver. He was happy to take the gold so hopefully he'll take more and drive us back to the farmhouse.

Robert   I can't spend my gold at Uncle Paul's stupid farmhouse.

Jane   Well, we can't spend it here and if it gets much later the sun will set and then we'll be stuck here.

Robert   What?

Cyril   Yes, if that fairy means what it says the gold will vanish, won't it?. We must find that driver.

The children search for **Driver**.

> We're rich with gold
> But we didn't see how this wish would unfold
> Nice and shiny, value naught
> Things to see nothing can be bought
> Get us out of town it's not what we thought
> We're stuck, we're stuck with

Cyril   Find him?

The others shake their heads.

Cyril   Mary, Joseph and the stinking apostles!

Jane   Calm down.

Cyril   I am calm.

Jane   You're not.

Cyril   Well, what are we supposed to do, genius?

A sign appears: 'Fine Horses For Sale.'

Jane   Okay. Wait here.

Cyril   No, Jane. I should do this. It's time I stepped up as the head of the family.

Jane   But you're not head of the family.

Cyril   I am, technically.

Jane   But I'm the oldest.

Cyril   Yes, but you're also a girl. Girls can't be seen dealing horses. It's unsightly. Sorry Jane, but that's just the way it is.

Jane *seethes.*

Anthea *grabs* **Jane** *before she hits* **Cyril**. *She leads an apoplectic* **Jane** *away.*

Cyril *brushes himself down, composes himself, takes a step towards the sign.*

Robert *follows.*

Cyril   What are you doing?

Robert   I'm coming.

Cyril   No.

Robert   But you might need back up.

Cyril   I don't, Robert. Stay with the others.

Billy *emerges.*

Billy   Afternoon, boys. Lost your way have you?

Cyril   Yes. I mean no. Sorry. What I mean to say is –

Robert   Sir. Are you the owner of this fine stable yard?

Billy   That I am young man. Name is Billy Peasemarsh of Peasemarsh Stables. What can I do for you?

Robert   We'd like to buy a horse. A fine one. Fine horses only, please.

Billy   I dare say you would.

Robert   And a carriage. We'll also need a fine carriage to go with the fine horse, so we'll see some of those too if you've got them.

Billy *chuckles.*

Billy   Want to buy a carriage. (*Shakes head.*) Come on, run along before I get tired of you.

Robert   I'm sorry.

Cyril   Robert.

Robert   We've come here to buy a state-of-the-art horse and carriage, and we shan't be running anywhere until we have it, thanks.

Billy   Oh, so I should trot the whole stable out for your honour to see, should I?

Robert   Yes, that would be good.

Billy   Look, you. No one takes Billy for a fool, boy. No one.

Cyril   Sorry, Robert is –

Billy   No clown without tuppence runs rings around me.

Robert   Don't you call me clown. And as for tuppence, what do you call this?

Robert *turns out his pockets. Gold cascades on the floor.*

Billy *is stunned.*

Billy *seizes* **Robert** *and frogmarches him.*

Robert   What? Get off me.

Jane   What's happening? Get off him.

Billy   Been dragging little girls into it as well, have you? Thieving scumbags.

Cyril   Sir. Listen. This is all a misunderstanding.

Billy   You. Come quietly to the police and I'll let the girls go.

Anthea *bites* **Billy**.

Billy (*enraged*)   Right.

With superhuman force, **Billy** *bundles the lot of them into the police station.*

Billy   Police! I've caught some thieves, sir.

Inspector   Thieves?

Billy   You heard of any gold being filched? Any stately homes been ravaged of their heirlooms?

Inspector   No. Judy Myers' ferret has gone missing again but that's all that's happened all day really.

Billy   Well, I'm sorry to be adding to your workload now, Inspector. But I've uncovered a major theft operation.

Inspector (*eyeing the children*)   Right.

Billy   These kids, sir. They've been stealing. Gold. Hoards of it. Turn out their pockets, you'll see.

Jane (*realising*)   Sunset!

Billy   That one (**Robert**.), he's the ringleader.

Jane   No, Inspector, please don't. It's nothing like that.

Billy   Listen to that. Guilty conscience.

Jane   If I could speak.

Inspector   Well . . . Alright then. What do you need to say?

Jane Okay. So. The truth is, sometimes in life we ask for things, and we don't know what we mean by it. We ask for just desserts, and we get prison. Not custard. Or we ask for honesty and get half-baked truths. We ask for, for a fair crack at the whip but really a whip is horrible way to treat a horse and none of it seems fair at all, so what I'm trying to say is . . . to cut a long story very, very short . . .

The suns sets.

Inspector Not sure I follow.

Jane That was all actually. Yes. That's everything.

Inspector Right. Better turn out your pockets then. All of you. Come on.

The children turn out their pockets. The gold is gone.

Billy No. No no. They're hiding it. It's there. It must be. I saw it. It's –

Billy *man handles* **Cyril** *like he's trying to shake out loose change.*

Inspector Mr Peasemarsh.

Billy I saw it!

Inspector That's enough. Billy. Go home.

Billy But –

Inspector I know you've been under a lot of stress recently, but come on now.

Billy No, I –

Inspector You've turned up here with four innocent children, and a baby, exclaiming that they're thieving bandits. Don't make me investigate why you've done that.

Billy *nods.*

Inspector Why don't you go home, get a horse ready, and make a wrong right by driving these kiddies back home. It's dark now so they can't be left. And that would be doing me a favour. How about it?

Billy (*with difficulty*)   Yes, Inspector.

Inspector   Thank you.

Billy *goes.*

Anthea   Sorry to hear about the missing ferret, Inspector.

Inspector   It'll show up. Always does.

Anthea   I'll let you know if I see it.

Inspector   That would be kind.

You aren't from round here, are you?

The children shake their heads.

Anthea   We're from London.

Inspector   Ooh. London.

Ah. Here's Billy with his carriage. I'll be off home then. Goodnight.

The children pile into **Billy Peasemarsh**'s *carriage.*

This is a much smoother ride than earlier with **Driver**.

Silence.

Cyril   I say, this is a very fine carriage, Mr Peasemarsh –

Billy   Shuttup.

Cyril   Okay.

. . .

Billy   Woah. Out.

No Tea

Back at the farmhouse.

Paul   A police station. A police station.

Cyril   It's a long story.

Paul   I'll bet it is. I'll bet it's a story and a half.

Jane   We didn't mean to.

Paul   And that makes it alright, does it?

I cleaned the house for you. Got your rooms all nice. Spent hours in the kitchen making stew. Veggies cooked perfect, dumplings soft. There I was thinking, they'll be back any minute, back for their dinner what they were so keen for. But you weren't, were you? You were in town. Up to all sorts of no good, and with the baby.

Robert   We said we're sorry.

Paul   Your mother would be furious, you know that?

Cyril   Uncle, we are truly sorry, we promise we won't do it again, but that stew does sound delicious.

Paul   It was.

Cyril   And I know we're back late, but since we're here now, could we have some?

Paul   No.

Cyril   What?

Paul   None left to have. I was so busy looking for you the dog got in and ate it.

Horrified silence.

Anthea   But – But I'm – I'm – I'm –

Anthea *bursts into tears.*

Paul *is dismayed.*

Paul   Oh.

Jane   It's alright, Uncle. I think Anthea just misses home.

Paul   Right. Well. Not much I can do about that, is there?

Look, there's no stew, but there's bread. So you eat that and then it's straight to bed. All of you. And tomorrow – you go as far as the fields and no further. Alright?

It and The Audience (Anthea Sneaks Out)

It *emerges from the world of the play.*

It   So *that's* A Show, is it? And I'm . . . I'm in it.

Right. Okay.

I like the singing.

If I'm in it, does that mean – ? Can I do a Singing? A song? I'd like that. Yes, I want a song. That would be good because it seems that human beings have forgotten about Psammeads. Which is rude. Considering how many wishes and miracles you've been given through the ages. It's very ungrateful actually.

Perhaps a Sing, yes, perhaps that would help you remember. Because –

You (*Audience member.*), how many years does a Psammead live for?

It *quizzes the audience on their knowledge of Psammeads. Every answer the audience gives is wrong. This makes* **It** *increasingly indignant and upset:*

How many Sand Fairies are left on the Earth?

Have another go.

Wrong! Anyone else? What age do Sand Fairies reach their full potential?

Wrong. We're born great.

Right. How do I start the –?

It *is given a mic.*

What's this?

It *makes a noise in the mic and is thrilled at how loud and impressive it sounds.*

The **Minions** *accompany* **It** *for 'The Psammead Song'.*

How to describe the indescribable, the unquantifiable
The most sophisticated, complicated, under-rated beings
To humans with heads like hollow balls
Who go around like know-it-alls
And simply lack the wherewithal
To comprehend what they're really seeing?
Well I can try . . . .
A Psammead's an ancient creature with magic in its bones
Fabulous from toe to whisker – a fact once widely known
We were here before mankind when reptiles roamed the earth
And when you humans came along at first you knew the worth of a
Psammead —— Sand Fairy Sand Fairy
Psammead —— fluffy, not hairy
Psammead —— Sometimes kind of scary
We're the mystifying, edifying, wish-supplying fairies of the sand
At first you humans brought us juicy grubs and sweet flower nectar
You made statues in our honour and treated us like treasure
But as the years went on and on the gifts got less and less
There were lots and lots more children born, with wishes more complex for us
Psammeads —— Sand Fairy Sand Fairy
Psammead —— the workload's kinda scary
Psammead —— are all these wishes necessary?
We're the overtired, uninspired, slightly wired fairies of

the sand
Suddenly Children everywhere, making wish after wish
without a care
For my poor poor purple peculiar kind; it started to
drive me out of my mind
Granting wishes! (Wishes!)
Day after day got me,
Got me so tired I –,
Des-per-at-el-y, needed a breaaaaaaaa-k.
No no no, please no, don't make me sing it again
Psammead —— Sand Fair-ahhhhh!
Psammead —— make it stooooop!
Psammead —— please, no more!
I've had enough of this wishy stuff I'm going to jump
back in my stupid hole.

It's song is interrupted by:

Anthea   HELLLOOOOO! Hello! Excuse me?!

*It is sucked back into the world of the play. This is disorientating
and painful for **It**.*

It   What – ? Where – ?

Anthea   Are you alright?

It   Oh, it's you.

Anthea   You look awful. Do you always look like that when
you wake up?

It   What time is it?

Anthea   Dawn.

It   Dawn?!

Anthea   Yes. I've come early. And let me tell you how I've
done that because I think it will come in useful to you.

So when you go to bed, you lie on your back with your hands
by your sides. And then you say, 'I must wake up at five' – or
whatever time you want to get up – and then, as you're

saying it you push your chin on your chest and whack your head on the pillow five times. Like this.

Anthea *demonstrates.*

It   Right.

Anthea   So try that next time. You might wake up feeling less tired.

It   Okay.

Anthea   How are your whiskers this morning?

It   They're a little frazzled but not so clammy today, that's kind of you to ask.

Anthea (*reaching out*)   Can I touch one –

It   No!

It *slaps* **Anthea**'s *hand away.*

It   I expect you've come for a wish?

Anthea   Yes please. It was very impressive last time.

It   You think so? Alright.

But before we get on to that I want to ask you something. What is the thing you're on? The 'Hhholiday'?

Anthea   You don't know what a holiday is?

It   No.

Anthea   Holidays are when there's no school or work or anything, and you get to go somewhere else to have time off or free time.

It   'Free Time?'

Anthea   Yeah. You know, when you do what you want and not what people tell you to do. Except if it's Mother, of course. If Mother tells you to do something it doesn't count. But she's not here so . . .

It *stares at* **Anthea**, *trying to get its head around this new human concept.*

Anthea   Can I make my wish now?

It   Yes alright.

Anthea   Thanks. And if it's not too much trouble, can I make it now and it be granted after breakfast?

It   Depends. What is it?

Anthea *whispers it to* **It**.

It *grins.*

It   Yes. I like that one. Alright, it'll begin just after breakfast. Stand back.

It *performs its wish granting.*

Breakfast

Farmhouse kitchen.

Jane   This time I'm wishing.

Robert / Cyril   No.

Cyril   You've had your turn, Robert.

Robert   But –

Jane   Why can't I wish?

Cyril   It's not your turn.

Jane   Why not?

Robert   Because you'll wish for something boring and good for people and we'll have a rubbish time.

Overlapping:

Jane   You're so childish Robert. / And stupid. This fairy means we have power and with power comes morals and doing right by people, because we can make a difference. How can we look at ourselves in the eye when (*Etc.*)

Robert   / I'm not. No I'm not. Don't you say that to me, Jane. I just want to have a nice time on holiday. Why can't I have a nice time in this miserable countryside place? I deserve to enjoy myself don't I? (*Etc.*)

Cyril   You're both being ridiculous. The reason I should take charge of wishing is because none of you know what's good for us. We should be wishing for something that will set us up for the future and (*Etc.*)

Anthea *has appeared. Perhaps she is grinning.*

The other children's arguing peters out as they turn to look at **Anthea**.

Cyril (*suspicious*)   What is it?

Anthea   Okay, promise not to be angry but, well, the thing is

Jane   Anthea!

Anthea   I made the wish already.

Annoyance from the others.

Anthea   But it is a good one, I promise.

Cyril   What is it, then?

Anthea   Well, it's

Robert   What?

Anthea   I

Jane   Just tell us.

Anthea   I think it's happening.

Anthea, **Jane**, **Cyril** *and* **Robert** *begin to grow huge, beautiful and colourful wings. They are awestruck.*

Robert   Woah!

Cyril   A good wish. Actually. Yes. A very good

Jane   Do they work?

Anthea *flaps her wings. Perhaps she rises off the ground slightly. The others gasp.*

Paul *(off)*   You finished?

The children look at each other. Their uncle mustn't see this.

Robert   Quick, through the window.

Jane   What about The Lamb?!

Anthea   I told the Sand Fairy he shouldn't have wings.

Jane   Why not?

Anthea   He's annoying.

Jane *nods.* **Anthea** *speaks truth.*

Paul   Listen. I've got some sugar beet what needs digging.

Anthea, **Cyril**, **Robert** *and* **Jane** *scramble out of the window.*

Paul *enters.*

Paul   It's hard work for one, but if you'll give me a hand, we'll . . .

Paul *looks around the empty dining room.*

The Lamb, *abandoned, begins to cry.*

Paul *shakes his head. Picks up* **The Lamb**.

Paul   There, there. Just you and me, is it? How are you at wielding a pitchfork, eh? Come on then.

Wings

Music.

The Children *are outside trying out their wings. They're practicing taking off. It's exciting and fun. The following lines are suggested but additional lines may be found to capture the delight of whatever flying method is found.*

Anthea   Look at Robert!

Robert   Did you see that?

Jane   I think I can . . . Am I doing it? Yes!

Cyril   It feels like – It's how it must feel like to sail, except up!

Jane / **Anthea**   Up.

Music. The children fly. A flying dance. Something beautiful and ethereal.

After a bit, **Anthea** *breaks off from the group. A moment of* **Anthea** *testing her wings by herself.*

Anthea *spots something.*

Anthea   A ferret!

Anthea *lands.*

Anthea (*to the ferret*)   You've been missing, ferret. People have been worried. Come here.

Anthea *scoops up the ferret. She flies to* **Billy Peasemarsh**'s *stable yard: 'Fine Horses for Sale.'*

Anthea   Mr Peasemarsh?

Anthea *sets down the ferret and flies off.*

Billy Peasemarsh *appears. Looks around for the voice but sees no one. He sees the ferret, scoops it up, goes.*

Anthea *re-joins her siblings.*

Then at some point we hear the following, which the children shout as they fly.

Jane   The houses look like squares of chocolate, don't they?

Cyril   Yes. And the fields look like green and gold Battenberg cake.

Anthea   Anyone else a bit hungry?

Jane   Yes, and thirsty.

Robert Look, a church. Sometimes they have wells by churches don't they?

Cyril, **Anthea** *and* **Jane** *land.* **Robert** *is distracted, goes elsewhere.*

Cyril Can't see a well.

Anthea There's a bird bath.

Jane No. Gross.

Anthea Birds drink from it.

Cyril Yes, but we can't, Anthea. We'll get ill.

Robert *re-joins his siblings.*

Robert Everyone. I found a pantry at the clergy house. And in it there was custard pudding, and cold chicken, and tongue and pies and jam and a big syphon of soda water. And the window was open so basically I took some and –

Jane Robert!

Robert What?

Jane That's stealing!

Robert No it's not. All I did was take the bare necessities for life.

Jane Still stealing.

Anthea We could knock on the door and ask?

Cyril Stupid idea.

Anthea Why?

Cyril Um.

Cyril *gesticulates pointedly and his wings.*

Anthea They might think we're angels.

Robert There's no way Cyril is an angel.

Cyril Well, thanks very much.

Robert   How about, we write the vicar a note. We explain that we're hungry children – which is the truth – and all we've done is taken the bare necessities for life.

Jane   Leaving a note to admit that you're stealing doesn't make it not stealing.

Robert   But we're children! No one begrudges feeding hungry children, do they? They can't because that's evil.

Everyone looks at **Jane**.

Jane   Fine.

Jane *takes a notebook from her pocket and writes the note.*

While **Jane** *writes:*

Cyril   Where is it then?

Robert   Well, I have a pork pie here, but then I flew the rest of it up to the church tower so we can

Anthea *and* **Cyril** *take flight.*

Robert   No wait! Hurry up, Jane.

Jane   Shhhh.

Robert   If they fly up first they might eat it all.

Jane *writes.*

Robert   Remember to put 'the bare necessities for life' – that's very important.

Meanwhile in the tower:

Anthea   What's this?

Cyril   A soda water syphon.

Anthea   What's it for?

Cyril   Makes the water go fizzy.

Anthea   Why? That's so stupid. Who wants fizzy in their water?

Cyril   Give it here, I'm thirsty.

Jane *delivers the note.*

Robert *and* **Jane** *fly up to the tower.*

Now all the children gorge themselves. They say stuff like:

Anthea   Ooh chicken!

Cyril   This is heaven.

Robert   Cyril! Hands off that slice of tongue. I especially got that for me so don't you go eating it all.

Jane   I'd like some cheese. Where is it? Pass it here please?

Cyril   Where's that custard pudding gone?

Anthea   Sorry.

Cyril   Panther! You ate all of it?

Anthea   It was too tasty.

The picnic is finished.

The children sink into a food coma. **Robert**, **Cyril** *and* **Jane** *drift off to sleep.*

Anthea *gazes out from the tower. Bliss.*

But then the light changes.

Anthea *realises: the sun is setting. Her beautiful wings begin to dissolve.*

Anthea   Oh no oh no oh no

It is dusk and the wings have all gone.

Oh.

Cut to . . .

No Wings (a.)

. . . Downstairs in the church.

Vicar, *assisted by* **Megan**, *is organising church candles.*

Megan (*holds up candle*)   Christmas?

Vicar   Yes, I think so.

Megan (*holds up candle*)   Easter?

Vicar   I think so.

Megan (*holds up candle*)   Funeral?

Vicar   Pink might not be quite the right tone for –

Megan   Christmas?

Vicar   I think it –

Megan   Wedding?

Vicar   Well –

Megan   Weddings are for love and love hearts are pink. This has to go with weddings.

Vicar   Yes but sometimes the bride and groom like to choose their own candles. And oftentimes they like white because, well, because it's . . .

Megan   But then where does pink go?

Vicar   How about we pop it in the birthday box for now and –

Megan   The birthday box! Of course, the birthday box. You stupid stupid stupid stupid

Perhaps **Megan** *hits themself with the candle.*

Vicar   Megan, Megan, stop that. What have we said before about that?

Megan   What?

Vicar   You are one of God's children, Megan. You would never do harm to one of God's children now, would you?

Megan   No, vicar.

Vicar   Exactly.

Megan   I only do harm to sinners, vicar.

Vicar   Well – No, we don't do that.

Megan   Why not?

Vicar   Because we – We've been through this before, haven't we? What do sinners need? They need our . . .

Anthea / Cyril / Jane / Robert   Help!

Megan (*mystified*)   Help?

Vicar   Yes, exactly.

Megan   Did you hear that?

Vicar   Hear what?

Megan   Hear the . . .? If you didn't then . . . I've heard from God, vicar. I'm having my spiritual awakening.

Vicar   Are you?

Megan   God needs our help.

Anthea / Cyril / Jane / Robert   Help!

Vicar   What was that?!

Megan   Oh you do hear it. So, it isn't God then.

Anthea / Cyril / Jane / Robert   Help!

Vicar   Sounds like there are people in the tower. Who on earth could be –

Megan   I'll fetch my gun.

Vicar   What?

Megan   Don't worry, vicar. I've got a background in defence.

Vicar   I don't think a gun is necessary, is it? Megan?!

Megan *has found their 'gun'.*

Megan   Let's go.

No Wings (b.)

Back in the tower the children are waiting for help.

Cyril   So first we'll dehydrate, then we'll starve, then we'll die of course, and then our corpses will shrivel up so no one can even recognise our bodies, and then they'll never know what happened to us and we'll be –

Jane   Someone's coming.

Anthea   Told you.

Jane   Quick everyone – hide the food.

Cyril   What do we do with this?

Cyril *holds up the soda water syphon.*

Robert   Hide it!

Cyril   Where?!

Jane   Throw it out the window.

Cyril (*sarcastic*)   Oh, great idea.

Jane   It's incriminating evidence, Cyril.

Cyril   Even more incriminating when it falls on someone's head and kills them.

Jane   Just get rid of it!

Jane *tries to grab the syphon from* **Cyril**.

Vicar *and* **Megan** *are now the other side of the door.*

Megan   I hear fighting.

Vicar   Goodness.

Megan   It's pirates.

Vicar   Gosh, really?

Megan   Yep, gang of pirates, no question.

Vicar   My goodness. In the village?

Megan   Alright you sinners, trespassers, defilers of God's house, open up the door and surrender your weaponry.

Anthea   We can't!

Cyril   Shhhh, Anthea!

Anthea   What? That's the truth.

Megan   Can't, is it?

Jane   We don't have any weaponry.

Robert   The door's locked.

Megan   Likely story.

Vicar   Gosh, they sound very young, don't they?

Megan   Right. Step away from the door. I am armed, I am armed. And I am not afraid to blow your maggoty, little heads off.

The children panic. **Cyril** *shoves the syphon in his clothing.*

Megan *ushers* **Vicar** *back.*

Vicar   What are we doing?

Megan   Going in.

Vicar   In that case, I have the key here if you'd like to –

Megan *kicks down the door.*

Jane   Don't shoot, please don't shoot!

Vicar   My goodness!

Megan   Stay back, vicar.

Vicar   But Megan, they're children.

Megan   They might look like children, might smell like children, but I'm telling you – pirates.

Robert   We're not.

Anthea   I don't even know any pirates.

Vicar   How on earth did you end up in here?

Hesitation.

Megan   SPEAK!

Robert   We wanted to eat a picnic.

Cyril   No we didn't.

Anthea   We came to look at the bells.

Cyril   Yes.

Jane   And take in the view.

Cyril   Exactly.

Anthea   And then we fell asleep, and then it was now, and that is what happened, I swear it.

Vicar   Of course, child.

Megan (*pointing gun at* **Cyril**)   You. You're lying.

Cyril   I'm not.

Vicar   Megan.

Megan   I smell a porky pie and I smell it there.

Vicar   Perhaps, but put the gun down.

Megan   Spill it!

Cyril *cowers. As he does, the syphon falls from his clothing.*

Vicar   My soda water syphon.

Megan   Got you.

Cyril   Please, please don't shoot. I admit it. We took it. I mean *I* took it. I took the soda water and some food but only because we needed the bare necessities for life. And I'm sorry for what I did, truly, and if someone needs to go to prison for it then I shall, but please don't shoot me.

Perhaps **Megan** *loads the gun and takes aim.*

Vicar   Megan!

Megan   Told you he's a pirate.

Vicar   Yes but – Well you see I've just heard from God.

Megan   Did you?

Vicar   Yes, just now, and God says, don't shoot him.

Megan   Really?

Vicar   Yes.

Megan   You're sure?

Vicar   Yes. He was crystal clear about the no shooting. So . . .

Megan *lower the gun.*

Megan   God's wish is my command.

Vicar   Good, that's –

Megan   But. The matter is not settled, Vicar. If the door was locked and you had the key, how did these lot get up in here?

Vicar   Yes, that is a good point actually.

The children look at each other. What can they say?

Anthea   The truth is, we wished for wings. And we got them. So we flew up here but when the sun set the wings disappeared and so we got stuck.

. . .

Vicar (*unsure*)   Yes. Well, I think it's about tea time now. So how about we have a nice cuppa and a slice of cake, and use this opportunity to pray together. How about that?

Robert   Great idea, vicar.

Everyone clambers down from the tower positively affirming the **Vicar***'s tea and cake suggestion.*

They get to the bottom. Tea and cake appear.

The children feast on cake while the **Vicar** *preaches at them:*

Vicar   Sermon sermon God sermon give-thanks virtue sermon not-into-temptation sermon praise-the-lord! Moral lesson Jesus.

Sermon sermon lord-our-father daily-bread forever sermon Hallelujah! Now-and-always sermon Jesus amen.

Ah, excellent. My good friend Mr Peasemarsh has come to drive you back home. May the lord be with you, children. God bless.

Vicar *goes. The children, once again, climb into* **Billy Peasemarsh***'s carriage.*

Awkward.

Cyril   Really excellent of you to drive us again, Mr –

Billy   Shuttup.

. . .

Missing ferret turned up today.

Anthea   Did it?

Billy   Was like it dropped from the sky.

Anthea   Amazing!

Perhaps **Billy** *and* **Anthea** *exchange a look.*

. . .

Jane   We're very late, aren't we.

Robert   What do you think Uncle Paul will say?

Jane   Don't know.

Anthea   He was so cross the last time.

Robert   Do you think he'll beat us?

Cyril   Probably.

Jane   Really?

Cyril   Yes. I heard they do that on farms.

Misery and dread.

The carriage stops.

Billy   Out.

More Tea

The farmhouse.

Jane   We are so sorry, Uncle Paul.

Cyril   Yes, honestly. Time just got the better of us and

Paul (*carrying in tea time treats*)   Currant scones. Hot cross buns. Chelsea buns

Robert   And then it got dark and we didn't know where we were so

Anthea   Please don't give us a beating.

Paul   And last but not least – a lovely Victoria sandwich.

There it is then. Tuck in!

Anthea   I don't think I'm hungry.

Cyril Don't be silly, Panther. Course we are. Famished, aren't we. Mmmm.

The children force down food.

Jane Delicious.

Robert Yum.

Paul Good. So um. Yes. So. There's something I need to tell you.

Jane What's happened?

Paul Nothing. Nothing's happened. Well, not nothing but – You see the situation is – Well, it's complicated.

Cyril What situation?

Paul So, Jenny –

Jane Mother?

Paul Yes. So it's – It's like –

When the grass becomes thin and nutrient-scarce, a dominant sheep will lead the others to fresh pasture. Now that might involve finding a gap in the fence. Or it might mean crossing the railway tracks. What I'm saying is, sometimes to get what we want we have to take risks and –

Robert Has Mother been hit by a train?

Paul What?! No! Not explaining this very well, am I? Thing is. Your mother's movement has got her into trouble. Not a lot, just – It might be some time before you go home.

Anthea How much time?

Paul I don't know.

Cyril But more than two weeks?

Paul Yes.

Robert Three weeks?

Paul   I

Robert   Four weeks?

Paul   I don't know!

Robert   But. But I want to go home.

I want my toys, and our room and the train set. I want to hear motorcars and carriages, and smell chimney pots, and – I want Mum to tell us off for dirty hands at dinner, and Mum to tuck us in, and Mum to – And Mum . . .

Robert *is suddenly lost and very, very small. Perhaps he cries.*

No one knows what to do.

Cyril *goes to* **Robert.**

Cyril (*gently*)   Come along now. Let's go to bed.

Robert *nods.*

Cyril   Come on. Panther? Jane?

The children go. Except **Jane** *who lingers.*

Uncle Paul *sighs. He sits at his piano.*

Jane   What's happened to Mother?

Uncle Paul *stops; he's not alone.*

Jane   You can tell me. I'm old enough.

Paul   Don't you worry yourself, Jane. Everything will work out al –

Jane   Is she in prison?

Paul   –

Jane   She is, isn't it she?

She left me this.

Jane *takes out her letter.*

Jane   Here – (*Reading.*) 'It'll be an uncomfortable time but I'm ready for it. I can manage whatever they put me through, because I have you. I know you will always be looking after our family. You are the best and strongest Jane I could ask for and I . . .'

Jane *steels herself.*

Jane   'An uncomfortable time.' What does that mean?

Paul   Jane.

Jane   Does it mean they're hurting her?

Paul   She'll be alright, Jane. I'm sure of it. I'm sure because she's always been that way. Always known what she's doing, your mother, ever since she were a girl. Now don't worry. It'll work itself out. Go to bed and tell the others they'll be home within a month. I promise.

Uncle Paul *goes.*

Jane *goes.*

. . .

It   It's time for a break!

It *scuttles off to escape.*

Interval.

Act Two

It and The Audience (Part Two)

It *is revealed in its nest.*

It   What's going on? You're back? But you all went away. I thought A Show had finished. You mean there's more?

On realising it has more to do and more wishes to grant, **It** *has brief tantrum.*

I see what this is now. This is Free Time for you, isn't it? You're all getting Time Off Free Time. Sitting there not working, meanwhile I'm . . .

It *fumes.*

Right. I've had enough of this Ashow thing. Enough wishes. Enough work.

I think it's time I had a . . . holiday. Yes.

I've got a plan. I'm going to escape all of this, all of you. I'm going to finish with this Ashow. And you know what? I'm going to have fun doing it.

It *grins.*

Ready?

It *sends us back into the world of the story.*

Breakfast Wish

Morning at the farmhouse.

The Lamb *is crying.*

Cyril *is trying to calm him.*

Cyril   Shuttup. Stupid baby. I know you want food, I'm just looking for it.

Where's the porridge? Shhh shhh.

Where does stupid Uncle Paul keep the stupid, stupid porridge oats.

An arm appears with a bowl of porridge.

Thank you.

Cyril   *takes the porridge then realises, in horror, that it has been supplied by a disembodied arm.*

Cyril *reveals* **It** *who has been scoffing the porridge oats.*

Cyril *shrieks.*

It   Morning!

Cyril   What are you doing here?

It   This is delicious (*Oats.*)

Cyril   You can't be here.

It   Flaky. A bit like earwig shells. Except chewy.

Cyril   Give me that.

It   Is there any more of that honey soil? I like that.

Cyril   What?

It   The crystals.

Cyril   You mean sugar?

It   Where do you keep it? Is it in here? What's in here?

Cyril   No!

It *investigates the rest of the farmhouse kitchen. Perhaps this involves opening things, sniffing things, or brushing things with its whiskers which give it a different impression of the item.*

Cyril   Don't touch that. You can't – Put that down. Stop it (*etc.*)

Anthea   Morning – AHHH!

Cyril Shhhhhhh!

Robert Will Uncle Paul notice if we polish off the – No!

Jane Oh my God!

Cyril SHHHHHHH!

It How about some of that red sticky stuff? What do you call that?

Cyril Jam, but you can't have any.

Robert Stop it!

Anthea (*fascinated*) What's it doing?

Jane Why is it here?

Cyril I don't know.

Jane Get rid of it.

Cyril I'm trying.

It Thought you'd be pleased to see me. You're digging me up the rest of the time.

Anthea Sorry, Psammead. Would you like a cup of tea?

Jane / Cyril / Robert Anthea!

Anthea Oh.

It What's Acupatea, is it gooey?

Cyril Right. Where's Uncle Paul? We need to stop him from coming in for breakfast or he'll see the –

The Lamb's *crying reaches an epic crescendo.*

Cyril Oh Lamb! I do wish you would just grow up!

It *grins.*

Cyril No! I didn't mean –

It *grants the wish.*

It   There. Ooof, that was

It *recovers itself.*

Thanks for the flaky things. You can keep your jam and the cupatea.

I'll be off.

It *goes.*

Robert   Cyril!

Cyril   I didn't mean to!

Jane   Shhh!

The Lamb *has stopped crying. It is notably silent.* **Jane** *tiptoes nervously to the pram.*

. . .

Jane   The Lamb's gone.

Anthea   No!

Robert   You've done it now.

Cyril   Obviously it was an accident.

Jane   We have to find him! Now!

The children search for **The Lamb**. *As they do the space transforms into . . .*

Grown Up

. . . A sun-kissed country lane.

Lady Artist *appears.*

Lady Artist *stops. She does a quick sketch of the view – the Edwardian equivalent of an Instagram story.*

Hilary *appears, perhaps in* **The Lamb**'s *oversized onesie.*

Hilary *sees* **Lady Artist**. *Stops. Preens.*

Hilary   Gorgeous day.

Lady Artist *looks* **Hilary** *up and down. Ignores him.*

Hilary   I said a gorgeous day.

Exceptional view.

Steaming hot fox poo.

Artist   Where?!

Hilary   Ah. Hello there. I don't suppose you'd be able to help a fellow in distress?

Artist   In distress?

Hilary   Yes. I'm afraid I am rather lost.

Artist   Oh.

Hilary   I wondered, is that a map of the area?

Artist   You wish to see my map of the area?

Perhaps **Lady Artist** *pronounces 'area' as 'aria'.*

Hilary   The area, yes, if it isn't too much trouble.

Lady Artist *passes* **Hilary** *her map as if handing a bone to a rabid dog.*

Hilary   You are too kind. My deepest thanks, Miss . . .?

Artist   Lady Womblesnatch.

Hilary   A pleasure. Lord Hilary at your service.

Artist   Oh.

The children appear, hidden and out of earshot.

Cyril   That's him.

Anthea   Are you sure?

Cyril   Yes. It's our baby brother!

Artist   Have you ridden very far, Lord Hilary? I'm ashamed to say I've not been introduced to your family.

Hilary   We're in London.

Cyril   See!

Artist (*suddenly very interested*)   London. Really?

Hilary   Really.

Robert   What's he doing?

Cyril   I don't know.

Artist   Well that *is* far.

Hilary   It is. But I would say meeting you here has made every mile worth it.

Artist   You flatter me, Lord Hilary.

Robert   This is disgusting.

Anthea   What do we do?

Artist   Where is it you're trying to get to?

Hilary   Well now, you know I can't think. Because the only place I wish to be is in the finest dining room in town, so that I might enjoy your company a little while longer.

Artist   I would be delighted!

Hilary   Then please, allow me to escort you into town my Lady.

Artist   With pleasure.

Cyril   No no stop! My Lady, I'm sorry, you can't go with him.

Artist   What is this?

Hilary   I have no idea.

Cyril   This man is not what you think he is.

Artist   Hilary, do you know this scruffy little urchin?

Hilary   Absolutely not.

Cyril   Lamb, it's me. It's Squirrel.

Artist   What on earth?

Cyril   And I'm sorry, but you are not a Lord.

Hilary   How dare you.

Jane   You're an infant.

Artist   There's another of them!

Jane   That's the truth I'm afraid. Just look at what he's wearing.

(*To* **Lady Artist**.) Lovely hat, by the way.

Lady Artist *clutches her hat to her head as if* **Jane** *might swipe it.*

Hilary   This is the height of aerodynamic sportswear. It's all the rage in London, everyone's got one.

Anthea   You can't go to tea with our brother.

Robert   Yes, leave him with us.

Artist   Four of them!

Hilary   They're nothing to do with me.

Artist   They said brother.

Hilary   They're lying.

Artist   Good day.

Lady Artist *goes.*

Hilary *is distraught.*

Cyril   I'm sorry, Lamb.

Hilary   She was The One.

Jane   You only just met her.

Hilary   You've destroyed my life.

Cyril　Now calm down.

Hilary　*You* calm down.

Anthea　Lamb, don't fight.

Hilary　My *name* is Hilary.

Anthea　Yes but – Hilary, the truth is you're a baby.

Hilary　Do you want us to fall into poverty? Do you? Do you want to see me begging on the streets? For pennies?

Cyril　Now you're being very dramatic.

Hilary　You have no idea, do you. Stupid children. That was a good match. I could have raised this family up. Rescued us. From destitution. From disgrace.

Anthea　What's he saying?

Robert　Don't know. Gibberish.

Jane　Hope he doesn't actually grow up to be like this.

Robert　Yeah, he's such a loser.

Hilary　Right.

Hilary *seizes his bicycle.*

Cyril　Alright Lamb, where are you going?

Hilary　To the only place where I have any hope of getting on. Soho.

Jane　Soho! But that's in London.

Hilary　Do you happen to know which way it is to the railway station?

Anthea *points.*

Hilary　Good. Enjoy your tiny, pointless lives.

Hilary *goes.*

Robert　Good riddance.

Cyril   Robert!

Robert   What? He's horrid.

Cyril   He's a baby!

Anthea   Do you think it's our fault that he's horrid?

Robert   No, how could it possibly be our fault?

Cyril   Horrid or not he's still our brother.

Jane   And he'll be lost and alone when the wish goes at sunset.

Cyril   I know!

Jane   Don't you shout at me – Anthea showed him the train station.

Anthea   Actually I'm pretty sure the station is that way.

Points in opposite direction to where she sent **Hilary**.

This changes everything.

Cyril   Thank God.

Jane   We have to stop him getting on that train. At all costs.

The children scatter in search of their brother.

Music. The Hilary song.

During this the children try to intercept their brother.

Hilary *gives them the slip*.

Anthea   Lamb?

Robert   There he is!

Hilary   What is this? Not the railway station. All I can see is sand. Heaps of it.

Robert   Quick on that, aren't you? Listen, about earlier, look I didn't mean what I said, I was –

Hilary *scoots off on his bike*.

Anthea Oh.

Robert Great.

> Oh brother please don't go!
> We'd simply miss you so
> (Don't fuss, stay with us!)
> Oh brother let's be friends
> Please don't worry
> Stay with us in the quarry

Hilary *runs into* **Jane**.

Jane Lamb! I mean – Hilary.

Hilary You lot are insufferable.

Jane Wait! Please I won't keep you long. Look, I'm really sorry about Lady Wombleface.

Hilary Snatch!

Jane Yes, sorry. It's just I heard she wasn't a nice person and I didn't want you to get hurt.

Hilary It's not a question of getting hurt.

Jane Isn't it?

Hilary No! It's a question of getting ahead.

Jane Right, well I've just seen sign for an 'esteemed party'.

Hilary Party? Where?

Jane Back that way.

Hilary Hmmm. Well, if I can't hear the gramophone pumping from here it can't be any good. See ya.

Hilary *goes*.

> Wait, brother, please. Don't you trust all of us?
> When making big decisions take the time to discuss!
> We know you're displeased let us put you at ease
> Please be happy, let us change your nappy

Robert *and* **Cyril** *have found a sign pointing to the train station.*
They are arguing about which way to redirect it.

Robert   This way.

Cyril   No too obvious, he'll guess.

Robert   But we want him to go the opposite direction!

Cyril   I know but it should go more like

Hilary   Think I'm an idiot? I'll be going that way.

Hilary *rides off in exactly the direction the children don't want*
him to.

> Come back, brother, please don't leave us in this vein,
> How will we forgive ourselves if he gets upon that train?

Hilary *looks left and right to check he's given the children the slip.*

Satisfied he's alone, he sings his feelings.

Hilary *solo:*

> All I've ever wanted is respect
> But all I've had from siblings is contempt and mild
> neglect
> I long to be considered as a self-respecting person
> But the harder I try, the situation worsens
> Why do the young have such hard luck?
> Does the fact I'm cute mean I'll always be the buck?
> I won't stand it any longer, I'll forge my own path
> And if someone tries to cross me I'll destroy them like a
> shark – !
> And so to London I go (**Children**: *Oh brother please don't*
> *go!*)
> I'm going to leave this show! (**Children**: *Don't fuss, stay*
> *with us!*)
> I belong with handsome lords and ladies
> Instead of staying here and being treated like a baby
> So get me on that train! (**Children**: *Please don't leave us in*
> *this vein!*)

You common folk will never see the likes of me again
From the grime, I'll socially climb,
Ciao ciao, adieu, goodbye!

The sound of a train horn.

Hilary *goes to the train.*

The children, out of breath, charge after him.

The sun sets. The train pulls out of the station.

The children watch in horror.

But there lies **The Lamb***, a bundle asleep on the edge of the platform.*

Cyril *goes to him. Picks him up gently. Hugs him. Perhaps the others hug them both. From now on* **The Lamb** *must be cherished, not resented.*

The wind rises.

A storm is coming.

It and The Audience (Robert Sneaks Out)

It *is in its den, joyfully attempting to pack a suitcase.*

As it does this, it sings a little of The Psammead Song.

Psammead —— Sand Fairy Sand Fairy
Psammead —— fluffy, not hairy . . .

It   So I've been learning more about Holidays. They sound really good actually. One of your better human ideas. Well done.

My research said that on holiday you should take 'Beachwear'. Is this a good beachwear?

It *holds up a ridiculous human 'beachwear' garment.*

Would you wear this? How do you put it on?

Never mind. I'll just take it.

A sound of thunder.

A storm is coming. They're expecting six inches of rain in Edwardian England. But I'll be long gone. Thanks to that last wish.

Really got them in trouble that one. Got them locked inside. And if they're locked inside they can't dig me up to ask for any more wishes, can they?

There can't be anymore A Show if there's no one left to wish in it.

It *cackles.*

Thunder.

So no more wishes for them. And no more wishes for you. It's finished.

It *hums the Psammead song gleefully.*

Robert   Hello?

It   What?

Robert   HELLO?!

It   No.

Robert   HELLOOOO?!

It *is hauled unexpectedly back out of its den and into the play.*

Robert   There you are. I've come for a wish.

It   No!

Robert   You look awful.

It   You can't do this to me!

Robert   Don't try and back out of it now. We made an agreement.

It   But you're meant to be locked inside.

Robert   I know but I climbed through a window.

It *howls in despair.*

Robert   What's your problem? Okay, so here's the thing. Can we have two wishes?

It   Two?

Robert   I'll tell you why, yesterday's wasn't a real wish.

It   Yes it was.

Robert   No, it was a trick. It was sneaky and dishonest, so now you owe us yesterday's wish as well as today's.

It   But if I do more than one wish a day I get a migraine.

Robert   Well sorry, but also not my problem.

It   Wow.

Robert   So the first is, we want Uncle Paul not to notice what we've wished for.

It   That's not a wish.

Robert   Why not?

It   Human adults don't notice anything. They're too preoccupied by nonsense things that don't matter.

Robert   Really?

It   What's your wish?

Robert   Oh okay, so my other wish is . . .

It   . . . Yes?

Robert   I'm just thinking. (*To self – weighing up options.*) Train set. Gummy bears. A tiger. No, that's

It   Wish to be the size of an oak tree. That sounds fun.

Robert   No, that's stupid. Besides it has to be something for indoors.

Oh this is too hard! I can't think. Wish one of the others could choose inste – No, no I didn't mean –

It *grants the wish. The most intense theatricalisation of a wish granting yet. Perhaps there is a hint of fury to the wish granting this time.*

It *recovers itself.*

It   That was a lot. Never done one of those before.

Robert   What is it?

It   I think I need to lie down.

Robert   What have you done?

It   Lots of sharp things and darkness and . . . blood and

Robert   What?

It   Well, it was nice knowing you. Whatever this is, I hope it's not too painful.

It *staggers away.*

Robert   Wait, no. What was the wish? Come back!

The sound of galloping horses.

Robert   What – What's happening?

A thousand-strong mounted army charges past **Robert**.

A knight appears. This is **Jakin**. *His war outfit is a children's idea of a great knight or warrior of old.*

Jakin (*to his horse*)   Woah.

Robert   Oh no.

Jakin   What varlet is this?

Robert   I I I'm

Jakin   An informant!

Robert   What? No no no

Robert *is captured by* **Jakin**. *They are subsumed into the army.*

Knights

A war camp. **Jakin** *and* **Robert** *stand outside the tent of a great leader.*

Robert   Where am I?

Jakin   Silence. You will not speak until questioned.

Robert   Okay.

Jakin   You will not meet his gaze.

Robert   Whose gaze?

Jakin   Behold our glorious leader. Sir Wulfric de Talbot.

Wulfric de Talbot *is revealed – a knight so sinister and terrifying, that an ice wind follows wherever he goes. He is majestic, cold and otherworldly. He is death itself.*

Perhaps his face is concealed in a great helmet, or if not then perhaps his voice and expression give little away about what he thinks and what he might do.

Jakin *stoops low.*

Jakin   My Lord. I present to you this wretched knave. A hostage of the besieged.

Wulfric *stares at* **Robert**. *Perhaps we hear his breath, deep and rasping.*

Wulfric *turns to* **Jakin**. *He nods. Once.*

Jakin   Whence comest thou and what is thine intent?

Robert   What?

Jakin   Speak.

Robert   I I I'm called Robert and I'm no problem, not any sort of problem at all.

Wulfric *breathes.*

Jakin   My Lord?

Wulfric *grunts.*

Jakin   What is thine errand?

Robert   I I

Jakin *draws his sword.*

Robert   My *gosh*, that's a big sword.

Jakin   Unfold thy tale or be drawn and quartered.

Robert   Tale, my tale, yes. Well, the fact is, basically The Cause got Mother into trouble, so she couldn't take care of us, and we got sent here, and then we found a Psammead, and and –

Perhaps when **Wulfric** *speaks, his voice is deep and like no voice we have ever heard before.*

Wulfric   Psammead.

. . .

Jakin   What is this, sammyad? A weapon.

Robert   No, not a weapon. More of a fairy. You could wish for a weapon but –

Perhaps **Jakin** *puts his sword to* **Robert**'s *neck.*

Jakin   Show it.

Robert   No no, no weapon. No sort of weapon at all, I swear. Please let me go. Please. I'm too young to be killed. I'm only seven.

Wulfric *breathes.*

Wulfric   Where wouldst thou go, boy?

Robert   Home.

Jakin   To the castle? To carry word to our foe?

Robert   What? No. Sir knights, my home is a farm.

Jakin   My Lord, methinks he doth feign innocence to entice thy mercy.

Wulfric *grunts.*

Jakin   We could release the knave if we first blind him

Robert   Please no.

Jakin   Or we could cut out his tongue.

Robert   No no please. I won't speak, I won't say a thing I swear. Please.

Wulfric *breathes.*

Wulfric   Boy. Go.

Robert   Oh thank you, my Lord, thank –

Wulfric   Return to the castle. Speak with our enemy. Tell them – Wulfric de Talbot cometh. Say he resteth not 'til every sword is bloodied, every foe, slain. Heads shall be severed from bodies. Tell them – this is thy end.

Take him.

Jakin *escorts* **Robert** *through the war camp.*

Robert   Wait, where are we – ? Is this a moat?

Jakin *throws* **Robert** *into the moat.*

As **Robert** *struggles in the water, the space begins to transform with the help of* **It**'s **Minions**.

As the space transforms, **Wulfric** *addresses his great army of terrible knights.*

Wulfric   Great warriors of my kingdom. Let us seizeth our territory. Rip limb from miserable limb. Splay their innards o'er the walls of this fortress. Let vultures pick at their skulls. Let maggots feast on their brains.

Show them no mercy.

It is time.

Wulfric *produce a great battle horn. He blows it. It's deep sound echoes through the army.*

Wulfric *disappears.*

The Siege

Cyril, **Jane** *and* **Anthea** *are at the castle with* **The Lamb**.

Anthea   There's hundreds of them!

Jane   Maybe thousands!

Anthea   How many would you say, Squirrel?

Cyril   I'd say at least three thousand knights.

Anthea   Wow!

Cyril *bounces* **The Lamb** *excitedly.*

Jane   Do you think they'll speak English?

Cyril   Yes Jane, obviously. Everyone speaks English.

Robert *appears dripping wet and exhausted.*

Robert   Who wished it?

Cyril   Don't know exactly.

Robert   But someone must have.

Jane   I think we all did.

Robert   What the hell was it then?

Cyril   Well, I quite fancied a fifty room castle.

Anthea   I wanted an epic battle.

Jane   And I wanted to meet a new culture of people, so . . .

Robert   Oh no no no

Cyril   Together we've made the best wish yet!

Robert   This is terrible.

Cyril   Don't be a grouch. Their war camp's incredible.

Jane   And it's a much more equal society. Look, all the women are putting on armour and helmets and –

Robert   No, listen. They're going to attack us. There's going to be a siege.

Cyril   Well, it wouldn't be much of a battle if they didn't.

Robert   But

Anthea   It's fine, Robert. We've got these.

Anthea takes aim with a child's bow and arrow.

Robert   No no you don't understand! I've seen them. They have huge, real weapons. And horses, and armour. They want to maim us, and tear our arms off, and put our heads on sticks. Honestly. I heard them say it. They were so fearsome I longed to wish for everlasting peace, and I hate peace!

. . .

The children look at each other – the situation starts to feel very real.

Cyril (*weakly*)   Right.

The sound of **Wulfric**'s *great battle horn.*

Robert   Oh God, they're coming.

Jane   What do we do?

Cyril   We need a strategy.

Jane   Okay.

Cyril   War strategy. Yes. They attack, I say we attack back.

Anthea   What?

Cyril   That's the last thing they'll expect.

Jane   But Cyril, there are thousands of them.

Anthea   What do we attack with?

Cyril   Rocks.

Robert   Rocks!?

Cyril   Sticks. Brooms. Mops. Chair legs.

Jane   That's not a good idea, Cyril.

Cyril   Yes it is.

Robert *whimpers in exasperation and fear.*

Cyril   You see our tactic is surprise. Jane and I can meet them head on and commence parlance with their leader. Anthea and Robert, you will attack from the right. Or the left. Or the right and the left – yes, there's two of you, aren't there, good.

Anthea   But –

Robert   I can't!

Cyril   Yes you can. Chin up, Robert, it'll be – Yes, it'll . . .

Anthea   Cyril. I don't think you should be war general.

Cyril   But I have to be. This family is my responsibility.

Anthea   Yes, but

Robert   I agree. It should be someone else. I think it should be Jane.

Cyril   Right. I . . . I see.

Not been very good as head of family, have I? I've been useless.

Jane   There is no 'head of the family', Squirrel. All there is, is us, and knowing what to do. And right now, I do know what to do. So I just need you to listen to me. Okay?

Cyril *nods.*

The great battle horn sounds again.

Jane   Right, quickly! The new strategy is this: we go hard on the defensive. Time is on our side, remember? If we can hide out in the keep until sunset, the wish will end and then all of this will disappear. Robert?

Robert   Yes, Ma'am.

Jane   Not Ma'am.

Robert   Chief?

Jane   Yes, I like chief.

Robert   Yes, Chief.

Jane   Okay. So first we need to barricade the doors and windows – anywhere that might be breached. Then we need to find weaponry. Proper weapons ideally, or if not then anything heavy that we hurl at them. Got it?

Robert / Anthea / Cyril   Chief!

Jane   Okay!

Music.

The children secure their castle and find weaponry.

Every available object in the space should be rearranged during this process.

Then the children head up to the keep.

Another horn sounds.

Jane   Alright what weapons have we got?

Anthea   So there's this fire poker, that's quite good, and we got some pots, lots of pots, a broken vase with sharp edges, and a steel capped boot.

Jane   Is that it?!

Anthea   Well – Yes.

Jane   What about swords, armour – proper weapons?

Cyril   We couldn't find the armoury.

Robert   But there must be one somewhere.

Cyril   Either the Sand Fairy didn't give us one or it put it somewhere hidden.

Jane   Is that a chamber pot?

Anthea   Yes. Cyril had to go.

Cyril   Anthea!

Jane   We might all need to go at some point.

The horn sounds again.

Robert   Look!

Wulfric de Talbot *can be seen in the distance. A great looming figure.*

Robert   We are actually all going to die.

Jane   No we're not.

Robert   We are. The Sand Fairy warned me. It said there would be blood and and – It said it would be painful.

The Lamb *starts to cry.* **Jane** *comforts him.*

Anthea   Do we come back to life when the wish ends?

Jane   I don't know, Panther.

Cyril   But surely

Jane   We don't know.

Wulfric de Talbot *advances.*

Perhaps he moves through the audience in a great, one-person, Norman warship. Perhaps he unveils a cannon which he loads and fires himself.

The effect should be one of **Wulfric** *advancing on the children's castle in a terrifying, spectacular fashion.*

Perhaps at this moment, **Wulfric***'s voice is disembodied from his physical form and sounds loud and deep and booming across the whole auditorium:*

Wulfric   I smelleth thy blood. Thy guts. I'll eateth thy gizzards. Tear thee limb from limb. Take thy skulls for trophies. Yes. I cometh. Sir Wulfric de Talbot cometh.

Jane   I didn't think I'd ever say this, but if we do die, I'm glad we're here together.

Anthea   Me too.

Robert   Cyril, you're not useless. You're the bravest, loyalist brother I could wish for.

Jane   Agreed.

Cyril   Jane, I'm sorry. I think you're brilliant. I just always got bogged down in feeling I was stupid.

Jane   It's okay. Panther. You're not weird. Well, maybe you are, but you're also wise and I –

Anthea   I don't miss Mother when I'm with you.

Wulfric   Fire.

Something is fired.

The children scream.

Wulfric *is at the foot of the keep. He is almost upon them.*

Jane   No. We must stop this. We're so close. Think!

Robert   The chamber pot. Pour it on his head!

Jane   Yes! Quickly.

A couple of the children pick up the chamber pot.

Robert   That's an awful lot of you know what in there Cyril.

Cyril   Shuttup.

Jane   Concentrate. One. Two. Three.

The sun sets. **Wulfric** *disappears.*

As the chamber pot is poured, **Uncle Paul** *returns from his farmyard chores. The contents of the chamber pot cascade over his head.*

Everything stops.

. . .

Jane   Uncle. I'm . . . I'm so sorry. We . . .

Paul   My house. Look at my house.

The children do. Now that the castle has dissolved with the sun, they see the farmhouse kitchen is in ruins.

Paul   My cooking things.

Robert   It was an accident.

Paul   My piano. What have you done to my piano?

. . .

Cyril   Look, we're very sorry, Uncle, but it can all be sorted out. Can't it?

I'll write to Mother and explain and if money's hard up then when we're home I'll get a job or, or I'll make my fortune as a man for real this time and

Paul   You don't see it, do you?

You're not going home.

Cyril   Of course we are.

Paul   If you do go back to London, it won't be that house.

Robert   Where else would it be?

Jane   You promised we'd be home within a month.

Paul   Who do you think pays the lease on it then? Because I can't pay it.

Cyril   Mother's writing pays the lease.

Paul   Your mother no longer has her writing. You don't get paid to write in prison. And she's sick. They've made her very, very sick, with their tubes and their contraptions and their forcing her to eat. And I can't write to her. Or I can but I don't hear back. So I don't know if she's reading them, or if she's better, or if she's worse. I don't know anything. And I'm sorry to tell you all this. Your mother would hate me for it. But I can't help it. I don't know what to do. Because I can't keep you. I can't be a parent. I'm rubbish at it. Look at this. Look at you.

I just – I don't understand you. I don't understand you at all.

Uncle Paul *goes.*

. . .

Robert   I wish The Cause would go to hell.

Jane   Robert!

Robert   What?

Jane   Take that back.

Robert   Everyone thinks it.

Jane   They don't.

Anthea (*quietly*)   I do.

Cyril   The Cause is very important to Mother, Robert.

Robert   Why? What good is The Cause it if it takes her away, if it makes her sick?

Jane   It's not The Cause that's making her sick, it's the prison guards and the government.

Robert   Well if she didn't have The Cause then she wouldn't be in trouble in the first place. So it's her fault, it's all her stupid fault.

Jane   Don't you dare say that. Mother's doing this for us, remember? It's for everyone. She wants to make a better world so when we grow up we can

Anthea   I don't care I don't care I don't care I don't care I don't care

Jane   THEN YOU'RE STUPID!

. . .

Jane   Panther, I'm

Perhaps **Anthea** *goes to put her arms around* **Cyril***.*

Jane   They'll win, you know? They've got to.

. . .

Cyril   Jane, what do we do?

Jane   I don't know.

Cyril   If Uncle Paul won't keep us. What happens? Where do we go?

Jane   We'll think of something. In the morning, we'll . . . .

The Last Wish (a.)

The children are with an exhausted **Uncle Paul** *in the ruins of the farmhouse kitchen.*

Jane   We need to tell you something. We're sorry we haven't explained before, but it's hard. Either people think we're lying, or they don't listen. But this is the truth.

Paul   Okay.

Jane   Are you listening?

Paul   Yes.

Jane   If you could wish for anything, what would it be?

Paul   Wish?

Jane   Yes.

Anthea   But the wish only lasts for one day and everything to do with it vanishes at sunset.

Paul   Right. Well. I don't know. A new barn would be nice. Oh but then it would vanish. Fifty pork chops. Oh – a Bechstein grand piano.

Jane   So the thing is, one day we went to the quarry and we accidentally dug up this Sand Fairy.

Paul   A fairy?

Jane   Yes.

Anthea   A Psammead.

Jane   But it's not what you think, it's

Robert   You see I struck up a deal with it, so it would give us one wish a day. And that's where we've been all the time. But then the wishes don't always go to plan, and so that's why we're often late back.

Paul   Right.

Jane   Do you believe us?

Uncle Paul *looks at them all.*

Paul   Well it's . . . You seem serious about it.

Jane   Okay.

You see I've made this plan. To fix everything.

The plan is, we go to the Psammead and we strike a new deal. We offer to give up our wishes until the end of time, if the Psammead promises to set Mother free, and repeat that every day for the rest of her life.

Anthea   So sorry, Uncle, but that means no pork chops.

Paul   Right, no that's

Anthea Or grand pianos. Though those were very good wishes.

Paul Thank you.

Cyril We could ask for an extra wish. How hard is it to grant a few pork chops?

Jane No, sorry, but we need to keep it simple. If we ask for too much, it'll get in a mood and just say no.

Anthea / Robert Agreed.

Cyril Agreed.

They look at **Uncle Paul**.

Paul (*realising he needs to say something*) Agreed.

Jane Good. That's it then.

Paul Can I –?

Jane Yes?

Paul Could I come with you?

Jane *looks at the others*.

Jane Alright.

The Last Wish (b.)

The children and **Uncle Paul** *go to the quarry and hunt for* **It**.

Jane Was it here?

Robert No, along a bit.

Anthea It was here the time before.

Cyril Anything?

Robert No.

Paul What does this thing look like?

Anthea   Purple. Long whiskers.

Cyril   Eyes on stalks.

Robert   Like a snail.

Paul   Right.

Eyes on stalks . . . Whiskers . . .

They hunt.

It *can't be found. Immense disappointment.*

Cyril   It was here.

Anthea   Was it?

Cyril   Definitely.

Paul   Maybe it just doesn't feel like it today.

Jane   You don't believe us.

Paul   No, I do. I –

Robert   It grants children's wishes. That's its only job.

Perhaps **Jane** *starts digging.*

Cyril   It's scarpered, hasn't it?

Robert   Little sneak.

Paul   Doesn't it like granting wishes?

Anthea   Not sure it does.

Cyril   It can get pretty crusty when we ask for one.

Robert   Well crusty or not it's not here, so

Jane *chucks down the spade in frustration and despair.*

Jane   I don't know what to do now. About any of it. It's hopeless. Everything is hopeless and useless and pointless –

Paul   Jane

Jane   Well, it is, isn't it? No use pretending otherwise.
That's the truth of it.

. . .

Paul   You know. If your mother was here, I don't think
she'd want you to make that wish.

Jane   But she's in prison.

Paul   Yes but for Jenny, it's not being in prison that's the
problem. Not seeing you, that's a problem, of course it is.
But I think, for your mother, if she were allowed to walk free
every day, while other women suffered in jail, I don't think
she'd think that was fair.

Jane   Then the wish is for The Cause to be won. That's it.
Then all of this would be over.

Paul   So The Cause is won but only until each sunset?

Cyril   I don't think she'd be happy with that either.

Paul   One thing I know about your mother, she doesn't do
things by halves. She wants change – real change – that will
last. Well that sort of thing, it takes work. People have to
understand what it means. And why it matters. If they don't
know why it matters, then what's to stop them changing it
back again?

Jane   Then . . . I don't understand. What's the answer?

Paul   To what?

Jane   Everything, the future.

Paul   I don't know. Not clever enough for that. But I'll tell
you what I do know. If a living thing is going to thrive and
be happy, it needs the right habitat.

So if you're a newt, you need . . .?

Anthea   A pond!

Paul   If you're a cow, you need . . .?

Cyril   Milk!

Paul   Pasture. Exactly.

But for children, I don't know about that. So for now, while this goes on, I need you to help me. How do we make this place your home?

Endings

Uncle Paul *plays the home-building song: a piece of piano music that the singing grows out of. Perhaps first* **Uncle Paul** *sings, and then the children join with wordless harmonies.*

> More than a roof set upon stacks of stone
> More than any four walls on their own
> Whether you live in the country or on a crowded street
> In the warm of the summer, or in winter's snow and sleet
> It doesn't make a difference when what makes a house complete is each other
> That's what makes a house a home.

As they sing, the children go back to the farmhouse with **Uncle Paul** *and together, as equals, rebuild the farmhouse kitchen, but with added touches that please each of them. Perhaps they redecorate* **Paul**'*s piano and string up a banner that says 'Bechstein Grand Piano' on it. Perhaps they put a framed photograph of mother on top of the piano.*

Towards the end of the song, **It**, *suitcase in hand, sneaks through the auditorium.*

It   'Scuse me. Coming through. I've got a Taxi? Yes, something called a Taxi is waiting for me. Oh. Just one more thing.

It *writes on a postcard. Then* **It** *picks out a child from the audience.*

You. Yes. I need a favour.

It *instructs the child to take the postcard to the stage and put it next to* **Anthea.**

It *goes. The song ends.*

Anthea *sees the postcard and picks it up.*

Anthea   Everyone!

Jane   What?

Anthea   I found something.

Robert   It's not a spider, is it?

Anthea   No. It's a postcard.

The children crowd around.

Cyril   Wow! In colour! Must have been expensive.

Anthea   It's a building.

Robert   It's a palace!

Cyril   No, it's a ship.

Jane   Let me see. Yes look, Cyril's right, that's the sea.

The doorbell goes.

Paul   I'll get it.

Uncle Paul *goes.*

Robert   What does that say?

Jane *(reading)*   'Saga Cruises.'

The children pull a face.

Cyril   What's the message?

The postcard is flipped.

Jane *(reading)*   Today only. Regards.

Robert   Regards who?

Jane   Doesn't say.

Robert   Stupid. Who puts 'regards' and then doesn't write their name?

Jane   Shhhh!

Anthea   What?

Jane   I heard a voice.

Cyril   It's Uncle Paul at the door.

Jane   No it's – It's . . .

A figure in the doorway.

Anthea   Mother?

Holiday

Music. The Holiday Song.

A grand finale. We are transported to a glamorous cruise ship where **It** *is enjoying its first ever holiday.*

It   At last! I'm on Hhholiday!

Time off. Free time. No wants. No wishes. No human children! Just . . .

What's this?

Perhaps **It** *is being offered something on a tray.*

Honey soil? Yes, I'll take some of that please, yes . . .

It *squeals delightedly.*

It's perfect. Magic. A wish of a lifetime come true!

> I was tired, so tired
> I needed a break
> I had blisters on my whiskers
> And an eyestalk ache
> I felt teased, so squeezed
> Of wishes granted

And frankly quite surprised
At what those children demanded
So I said don't let them drive you mad, you old
Psammead,
Yeah, you can do whatever you choose.
So I found a thing called a brochure
And I said: here we go sir
I've got nothing at all to lose,
I booked myself on a cruise!

It's my time, my time
There's just so much to see
From the squishy, cushion lounger on my balcony
And I'll wave as we leave, the harbour dock,
Before putting on my very finest fairy frock
Yeah I'll tuck in a napkin as I dine with the Captain
Before indulging in an afternoon snooze
I'll have a beetle martini with a starfish panini
Yeah you know I don't need an excuse . . .
I booked myself on a cruise!

End.

Printed in the USA
CPSIA information can be obtained
at www.ICGtesting.com
LVHW050851060324
773713LV00001B/66

9 781350 423121